Hidden Gems of the Bible

Say and Pray

Affirmations for a Better Life

By Phyllis Cook

Copyright page

(KJV) King James Version

Most scripture quotations are taken from THE KING JAMES VERSION and is listed as Public Domain.

(NKJV) New King James Version

Some scripture taken from THE NEW KING JAMES VERSION®. Copyright © 1982 by Thomas Nelson, Used by permission. All rights reserved.

(NIV) New International Version

Some scripture taken from THE HOLY BIBLE, NEW INTERNATIONAL VERSION®, NIV® Copyright © 1973, 1978, 1984, 2011 by Biblica, Inc.® Used by permission. All rights reserved worldwide.

COPYRIGHT © 2024 PHYLLIS COOK

Author and Publisher

All rights reserved! No part of this book may be reproduced in any way or form without permission of the author and publisher.

2 Corinthians 1:20

"For no matter
how many promises
God has made,
they are "YES" in Christ"

About Hidden Gems of the Bible

The bible is like a roadmap with hidden treasures spread throughout its pages. It contains the most valuable gems that anyone could possess. These valuable gems are the promises (phrases and statements) inspired by God himself. These sayings can be life changing!

They make wonderful affirmations or declarations to say and pray. They help in our efforts to reach out to our creator; they encourage and lift our spirits; they help to increase our faith. They give us peace of mind as we apply them to our own lives!

I believe God's words are carriers of power that we can apply to our own lives.

The bible is full of these great treasures. There are promises for love, hope, generosity, forgiveness, protection, deliverance, wisdom, understanding, prosperity, health and healing. My book gives some of these promises as it goes into detail of how and why they can work for the reader. I have also included bible affirmations to say and pray.

HIDDEN GEMS OF THE BIBLE

Affirmations for a Better Life

Table of Contents

Copyright page 1
2 Corinthians 1:20 2
About Hidden Gems of the Bible 3
Author Opinion and Introduction 6
Giver of Life 8
God's Faith Works by Love 10
Love has a Voice 15
Words are Carriers of Power 17
Envy Gets in the Way of our Peace. 22
Forgiveness 25
Making Changes for the Better 29
Quantum Entanglement 31
Protection 38
Wisdom, Understanding, Prosperity 41
First Fruit of the Spirit 47
Stopping the Voice of debt 62
Health and Overall Well-being 66

Affirmations 78
Giver of Life 79
God's Faith Works by Love 79
Love has a Voice 80
Words are Carriers of Power 81
Envy Gets in the Way of our Peace. 85
Forgiveness 85
Making Change for the Better 86
Quantum Entanglement 87
Protection 88
Wisdom, Understanding, Prosperity 90
First Fruit of The Spirit 92
Stopping the Voice of Debt 96
Health and Overall Well-being 97

Author Opinion and Introduction

The Bible is God's way of communicating with us. As we read it, hear it, and speak it for ourselves, it helps us in building a strong foundation of faith. God's written words can inspire us to believe in him for anything and everything that pertains to the good life that he wants us to have.

I believe laws of physics come into play when we work on building our foundation of faith. Knowledge can come from both good and evil sources. To live a happy and healthy life, we have to fill our minds with the right stuff, now! We can create within ourselves a mindset of success in every area of our lives. We can actually make adjustments to our destinies through a fascinating law of physics referred to as Quantum entanglement.

So, if you want to change your destiny, you have to forcefully change your thinking. Affirmations do just that.

God is the giver of life and he is a God of love (1 John 4:8). Tear down any barriers that keep you from living a healthy lifestyle of victory, prosperity and real joy. Tear down any barriers through the words inspired by God for God loves you!

Giver of Life

The bible gives us answers to all of life's questions, and it is the doorway to our creator. It is the greatest book ever written and has been known to powerfully alter destinies.

We are going to briefly look into God's words of wisdom, his love and protection, as well as his stories of prosperity and healing. They can have a profound effect on our lives for the better. God's word creates in us the confidence, self-assurance and faith that we need to live a life of peace, harmony and overall well-being.

>All of God's promises to us are
>"Yes"
>In Jesus Christ!

"In the beginning was the Word, and the Word was with God, and the Word was God (John 1:1-3). The World was framed by the Word of God (Hebrews 11:3).

And the Word was made flesh and dwelt among us" in a human body (John 1:1,14).

As the offspring of God himself, Jesus became a literal human voice (or spokesperson) for the Father.

Prayer and affirmation using God's Word

Father, I believe that you give us all things richly to enjoy, for you are the giver of life (1 Timothy 6:17.

I thank you Father for all your promises. For no matter how many promises that you made, they are "Yes" in Christ" (2 Corinthians 1:20).

God's Faith Works by Love

<u>Faith</u> is the <u>substance</u> of <u>things hoped for,</u> and it <u>works</u> (or materializes) <u>by love</u>. **(Hebrews 11:1 and Galatians 5:6).**

These two scripture references reveal how to access God's blessings for a better life. Hidden gems about the kingdom of God are revealed throughout the bible. It is interesting to note, that Jesus lived and operated his ministry using this same faith principle, and so can we.

Faith and love originated out from God, for he is the maker and creator of all things, and he is a God of love (Colossians 1:16-17, John 4:7-16). If you want faith to work, you have got to have love, for, faith and love go hand in hand!

We can access God's faith for something that we are hoping for, from within ourselves. It all has to do with God's love for his Son, Jesus.

Jesus had and still has great love and compassion. He is our example of what faith and love can do together.

Let me explain!

The connection between God the Father and his Son is love. God loves Jesus, and Jesus loves his Father!

Jesus in his human nature, became the mediator between us and God his Father. He wanted his Father to give us forgiveness, deliverance and freedom from the effects of sin. He wanted his Father to give us love and eternal life. By his great sacrifice of love when he died for us, he brought into existence a new and perfect relationship for humanity. What he had asked God his Father for, was honored.

Jesus created a love connection or bond between us and his Father. He became the love connection for God to become our Father.

We became God's people through their bond and connection of love. If we bond with Jesus Christ, we are also bonding with God his Father.

If God who is Spirit loves his human son, then he loves us too. He wants to impart his love in all of us, but there are other outside forces competing with his love (Galatians 5:19-21). His love can reside within us because he gives it to us as a gift. He gives it to us when he gives us mercy, forgiveness and eternal life. He gives us his love, when he gives us his Holy Spirit.

The fruit of the Spirit is love, joy, peace, longsuffering, gentleness, goodness, faith, meekness, temperance: against such there is no law (Galatians 5:22-23). This is the fruit of his love, his character and his thoughts and feelings. The Spirit of God is all about love!

Love is powerful! The influence, impact or effect of God's love flows from within the dimensions of where he resides and exists. God can exist within us through his Holy Spirit. You could compare it to how alternating currents of electricity flow and exist. However, love is the most powerful power there is.

Jesus loves us and he loves God! The <u>love</u> between God and his earthly son is the greatest connecting force, power, or energy that we can have, in order to access the faith realm (1 Corinthians 13:13).

Jesus had great faith in believing his Father would honor his request. He had to trust his Father to raise him from the dead, after his death. He had to have faith in God and trust him with his life, and ours!

Jesus gave his life to save ours. God was well pleased with his faith and sacrifice of great love. His love was selfless! Greater love hath no man than this, that he lay down his life for his friend (John 15:13).

To sum it up, it is through the <u>love and faith</u> of Jesus Christ that we have access into the good things of God. He opened the door! It is all because of what he did! He loved his father and he loved us. Jesus was and is our greatest example of how powerful God's love is. He is our greatest example of how love and faith go hand in hand, together.

Faith is the substance of things hoped for, and it works by love. (Hebrews 11:1 and Galatians 5:6).

The <u>love of God</u> has been poured out in my heart by the Holy Spirit who was given to me. (Romans 5:5). God gave me his Love. God loves me!

The fruit of the Spirit is love, joy, peace, longsuffering, gentleness, goodness, faith, meekness, temperance: against such there is no law (Galatians 5:22-23).

I allow God to work in and through me by the fruit of his Holy Spirit.

God's love for me and in me is what activates faith for all good things (John 14:6, 12-18, 21-23).

Thank you, Jesus for I can follow your example of how faith works! Love and faith go hand in hand!

Love has a Voice

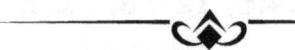

Jesus gave us the two greatest commandments. The first is to love the Lord God with all our hearts and with all our souls, and with all our minds. We can do this through Jesus Christ. This is the greatest command. The second is to love our neighbors as ourselves (Matthew 22:37-39).

Love is <u>patient</u>, love is <u>kind</u>. It does <u>not envy</u>, it does <u>not boast</u>, it is <u>not proud</u>. It does <u>not dishonor others</u>, it is <u>not self-seeking</u>, it is <u>not easily angered</u>, it <u>keeps no record of wrongs</u>. Love does <u>not delight in evil</u>, but <u>rejoices with the truth</u>. Love <u>always protects</u>, always <u>trusts</u>, always <u>hopes</u>, always <u>perseveres</u>. ...And now these three remain: faith, hope and love. But the greatest of these is Love (1 Corinthians 13:4-8, 13).

Love comes from God! He that loves not, knows not God for God is love! If we love and forgive one another, God lives in us. Loving and forgiving is something that we do rather we feel like it or not (1 John 4:7-18).

God's Love - For God so loved the world, that he gave his only begotten Son, that whosoever believeth in him should not perish, but have everlasting life. For God sent not his Son into the world to condemn the world; but that the world through him might be saved (John 3:16-17).

His Son Jesus - Greater love hath no man than this, that he lay down his life for his friend (John 15:13).

Love had a voice and it made a difference! The perfect love of God and his Son Jesus was faultless and unselfish! If God the Father and his Son Jesus took it upon themselves to love us, we ought also to love one another (1 John 4:9-11). Love has a voice and it makes a difference!

There is no fear, (or anxiety) **in love, and perfect love casts out** (forcibly expels or dismisses) **fear (1 John 4:18).**

I can do the two greatest commandments to love God above all and secondly my neighbor. The life I now live is by faith in Jesus Christ that is in me. I have the greatest love residing within me. I can do all things through Christ who loves and strengthens me" (Philippians 4:13, Galatians 2:20).

Words are Carriers of Power

In Isaiah 55:10-11 God said, "As the rain and snow come down from heaven, and do not return to it without watering the earth and making it bud and flourish, so that it yields <u>seed for the Sower and bread for the eater, so is my Word that goes out from my mouth: it will not return to me empty, but will accomplish what I desire and achieve the purpose for which I sent it</u>."

I thank you, God for your word! Your word shall not return to you unfulfilled, but will accomplish that which you please, and achieve the purpose for which you sent it.

According to your word, I ask that <u>your words that I speak</u> accomplish what I desire, and that it achieve the purpose for which I send it (Isaiah 55:10-11).

Jesus, you said that you came so that I can have life more abundantly (John 10:10). You also said that you are the vine and I am the branch. If I remain in you and you in me, I will bear much fruit like a tree with its branches.

If I remain in you and your words remain in me, I can ask whatever I wish and it will be done (John 15:1-7).

I give human voice to God's sayings, just like you, Jesus! I know that my giving voice to God's words links me to him through you. What I say shall accomplish that which I please. It shall prosper in the thing that I send it, because it was, and is, God's words first.

I believe that sound waves are powerful when given substance, direction and instructions. They can create change.

I know that I can speak or give voice to receive what I need and even want for God loves me and wants me blessed.

God is able to bless me abundantly, so that in all things at all times, having all that I need, I will abound in every good work (2 Corinthians 9:8).

In you Jesus Christ I have abundant life (John 10:10).

The world can be affected and shaped by the words of God's people. Words have power to affect the future. Just like God, we who are born again of his Spirit and made to be his children, are his little gods. We can curse or bless what happens next with our thoughts, if we speak them. Our positive or negative words and actions do cause some kind of reaction.

In the bible, there is the story of a woman who had a blood issue for 12 years. She used her own <u>imagination,</u> her own thoughts and <u>words</u> to receive healing from Jesus (Mark 5: 25-34, KJV).

> <u>In her imagination, she saw</u> herself being healed at the very moment that she would touch the hem of his garment. It was her point of contact.
> <u>Then she spoke</u> what she saw in the vision.
> <u>She acted out her vision</u> and received her healing instantly.

Every time I speak words of faith to make changes in my life, it creates a stronger image or imprint inside me, as I hear myself speak. The more I speak it, the more it is polarized and energized, until I know that I know. What I say sets up my future.

Life and death are in the power of the tongue. I choose to speak life (Proverbs 18:21).

A gentle and wholesome tongue is a tree of life, but willful words spoken against the word of God, breaks down the spirit (Proverbs 15:4).

I keep or guard my mouth and tongue, for it keeps my soul from trouble (Proverbs 13:3, 21:23).

I strive to let no corrupt communication proceed out of my mouth, but that which is good to the use of edifying, that it may minister grace unto the hearer (Ephesians 4:29).

My desire is to speak things that edify and improve my life and the life of others.

I am reminding myself to put a watch on what I say, and always strive to speak in love. I choose to speak words of life!

I create the fruit of my lips. I shall be satisfied with good, by the <u>fruit of my mouth</u> (Proverbs 12:14). I remind myself that all words are seeds that produce something. Good seeds produce good results.

Father, I confess and believe that your spiritual kingdom principles, your powerful life-giving seeds, are available to my spirit from yours (Luke 8:11-18). I confess that the Word of God is alive, living in me! For words are living things!

Out of the abundance of my heart my mouth can and wills to speak good things (Luke 6:45). All good things come from you, God.

Just like you did Jesus, I want to plant good spiritual seeds of love to reap good result. You said that you are in your Father, you are also in me and I am in you (John 14:16 and 20, Ephesians 3:17, Galatians 2:20, 4:19). You said we are connected as one together, so I can speak the will of our Father for my life to reap good results

I confess that as I walk in your ways Lord God, you make my way plenteous in goods, you open your good treasure, you bless all the work of my hand and I can lend to others and not have to borrow for myself (Deuteronomy 28:9-12).

Thank you for your words that give blessing to my life.

Envy Gets in the Way of our Peace.

See to it that no one falls short of the grace of God and that no bitter root grows up to cause trouble and defile many (Hebrews 12:15).

Envy is a negative energy force that can override our own good and positive thoughts and feelings. It steals our own peace of mind. It can rob us of feeling love, peace, joy and happiness. If we let it, it can hurt us!

Envy is a negative emotion that can occur when a person lacks or wants what another has. It can produce thoughts of resentfulness, hatefulness and jealousy. It can even generate rage.

The bible says judge not, that you be not judged (Matthew 7:1).

In the story of Cain and Abel (Adam and Eve's two sons), they both had presented different offering to God. Cain became very angry and jealous when he saw that God was more pleased with his brother's offering than his own (Genesis 4:5-8).

When God saw Cain's immediate response, he gave him some advice. He told Cain that if he did the right thing, it would be accepted. But if didn't do the right thing, sin would be crouching at the door waiting to be invited in. If he gave attention to the raging thoughts, they would come in and overtake him. God told Cain that he needed to take charge over it before it took control over him (Genesis 4:7).

Cain did not try to rule over it. Instead, he remained in a mindset of rage. He hung on to the jealously of his brother and it did overtake him, just like God said it would. He killed his own brother and was cursed for his actions. His rage affected his future in a bad way and ended his brother's life.

How do you rule over envy? First, recognize it as YOUR enemy. Then, take some kind of action for the better. Do something or speak something positive or walk away from the situation. Show kindness on purpose rather you feel like it or not, even though it may be one of the hardest things you have ever done. It can soften your own feelings of anger and keep you out of trouble with others. Rule over the situation! Practice ruling over it and keep in mind that it is the right thing you can do for yourself.

Choose to change the outcome for good. Don't make their circumstances be your loss. Don't let their circumstances dictate yours. Don't let the situation own your feelings. No matter how uncomfortable it may make you feel, strive to do good to others to make envy of no affect for either one of you.

We are all a work in progress! We can make things better for ourselves and others as long as we continue to move forward.

God is very forgiving for our shortcomings through his Son Jesus, so we should also be forgiving to others!

Regarding envy, I choose to change the outcome for good in any bad situation. Someone else's circumstance does not dictate my future, I do! Envy will not rule over my feelings, I will! I choose to make envy of no affect in my life or another by doing the right thing. I rule over it according to Genesis 4:7 because God said I could. I plan to keep my feelings of love, peace and joy and be happy.

Forgiveness

Forgiveness benefits everybody. It is a powerful weapon of strength against unpleasant feelings. It frees us when we choose to forgive, rather we feel like it or not. It helps us to go forward out from our own self-inflicted bondage of anxiety, that has been triggered by the actions of another. We must take control over our feelings. We must forgive others, as well as ourselves in order to sustain our peace and joy. We help ourselves when we forgive. It is an important part of God's covenant.

If we have trouble fixing the issue, then we can make it between them and God. Pray and release the other person or persons into God's care, for this is the will of God. Jesus said to pray for others, even those who have willingly done us wrong (Matthew 5:43-48).

We free ourselves when we take responsibility for our own feelings. The real enemy behind the scenes is Satan. He comes against us in thought. It is his intent to take control of our emotions, so he can rob us of our peace and joy. We free ourselves, when we reject or block his emotional weapons from ever taking root. We can reject or disrupt his plan by recognizing it, ignoring it, and forcing ourselves to think and speak differently, on purpose!

We don't have to necessarily tell another person that we forgive them, unless they need to hear it from us for their benefit as well. They may not even realize that there was an issue.

For though I live in the world, I do not wage war as the world does. The weapons I fight with are not the weapons of the world. <u>They have divine power to demolish strongholds</u> (2 Corinthians 10:3-4).

I demolish arguments and every pretension that sets itself against my mind, and the knowledge of God. I place these thoughts into captivity to the obedience of Christs (2 Corinthians 10:5).

Forgiveness is part of God's covenant with me. God forgave me and so I choose to forgive!

I choose to bring thoughts of unforgiveness and blame of another into captivity. I move forward out from any bondage. I take back my freedom from an unproductive situation.

I respond back with God's divine power that demolishes strongholds. I choose forgiveness and it sets my emotions free.

Transfer the thoughts of unforgiveness from your mind into the mind of Christ for captivity. How do you do it? Simply just imagine yourself turning it over to him. He is the greatest forgiver of mankind, and he can handle it. Scripture shows us that we can give our faults or shortcomings to him.

Always be prepared for a challenge just in case. Don't let negative emotions fester and ruin the rest of the day, like Cain let his rage ruin the rest of his life. Keep in mind that you harm yourself, if you don't let it go!

How can God bless us around others, if we keep thinking or saying bad things about or to them? How does that help us? How does it help in getting them to be a blessing in our lives instead of a curse, especially if we depend on their presence or services for that moment in time?

If we grasp the reality of who the real enemy is, it helps in nullifying the bad thoughts about the other person. It can also help us by affecting the way we treat them. In turn, it may even change their behavior towards us for the good.

We can practice our right of choice to do good in order to alleviate evil (Ephesians 4:26,27,29-32).

Making Changes for the Better

Just like God, we can destroy what happens next with our own words. We are God's little gods. If we ignore bad or unproductive thoughts, they can die unborn, especially if not spoken or acted on.

Firstly, we should not allow negative thoughts and/or other people to control what happens next in our lives. We can stop them from robbing our own power from us. If we don't let them dominate our feelings, then they won't.

Secondly, if at all possible, give niceness to get niceness back! We should reflect God's love even if we don't feel like it! We should persistently exhibit a good attitude. A negative attitude can be visible seen in our bodily gestures. We normally portray how we feel in our facial expressions and bodily stance, so practice smiling and look more approachable! We should strive to influence others to imagine good thoughts about us.

Thirdly, choose the right thoughts to speak and do. Good thoughts can die unborn if not spoken and or acted on. Plant spiritual good seeds. Say and do good things, on purpose! Do not plant angry seeds because evil spirits can get involved. The fruit of our speech rather we speak good or bad thoughts, give seed into our own lives. We can bless or curse our future as we speak. So, we should be careful what we say!

God, your word says to let the people praise you, then shall the earth yield her increase and you shall bless them. I praise you God as my own God. I believe in your word that says you shall bless me (Psalms 67:5-6).

Blessed be your name Lord for you hear the voice of my supplications. You are my strength and shield. I engage in and soak up your perfect and holy presence. I become strong in your strength. I trust in you, and I am helped. My heart greatly rejoices as I give you praise for all you do.

I want to think, speak and do the right thing, in order to affect my life, and the life of others for the better. I want to influence others to have good thoughts about me. I want to live in your blessing and not in the curse

Save us as your people, bless us as your inheritance, feed and lift us up together forever (Psalms 28:7-9).

Quantum Entanglement

Einstein says that energy cannot be created or destroyed, only transformed into another form of energy.

Quantum entanglement is where a cluster of particles interact with each other as one, even when separated by a vast distance. It doesn't matter the location, or difference in time and space.

Scientist believe that a pair of Photons separated by great distance seem to affect each other, when one of them is observed.

According to God's law, "the law of the Spirit", we can connect our spirit directly to his. Jesus is the direct link to the Father. He himself said that he was the way, the door or gateway between Heaven and Earth (John 10:7-9).

He said his purpose was to give us life to the fullest (John 10:10). Through and because of Jesus, we can draw wisdom, strength, comfort and healing. Through Jesus we have access to God's own Spirit of love and mercy for complete success.

We can approach God's throne with confidence in times of need, even though we are eons away from him in the natural sense (Hebrews 4:16).

God gave us an actual WORD, expression, or NAME that he responds to, when we need him. It is the name "Jesus". That name is above all other names to him.

Words that are spoken are containers of thoughts. The word "Jesus" is a container that God gave us, when he gave his Son.

Let me explain:

When we speak the name Jesus, it reminds God of the awesome deed that his Son did to save us. It carries good thoughts to God about his Son. It gets his love and attention.

Jesus means the world to him, and he listens when he hears the name of his Son. The name "Jesus" is the word responsible for the transport of information between God and man.

Jesus was referred to as the "Word of God" in the beginning before our world was even formed. Eventually, he was <u>sent</u> to earth to be born and live in a <u>bodily</u> <u>container</u> like ours until his death (John1:1-2, 14, John 17:3-5, 8).

Bodies are types of containers that house our spirits. If the Son of God can live in an earthly body like ours, then he could also live and exist within ours.

He was the part of the Spirit of God that was sent to live in us. He is also referred to as the Spirit of Christ (Romans 8:9). It has to do with Sonship. God adopts us as his children. We are connected to our maker through what Jesus did, when we accept his sonship status for ourselves (Romans8:14-15).

Words are spiritual containers that we can't see as we speak, but we can hear them from within through our thoughts. When we speak words, our words or containers carry our thoughts out into the world.

If Jesus is involved, spiritual substances can travel or flow in-between space and time at God's speed. There is nothing that can slow it down, because he is connected to both worlds, and he is very much alive.

We have a direct line, portal, gateway or <u>door of faith</u> if Jesus resides within us, no matter who we are (John 14:6 Acts 14:27 KJV). God is our Father and we are his children. Like attracts like! We have the connection through Jesus, the Son of God who lives within our hearts. What we say is connected to where it belongs.

Jesus has been here and returned back to his original origin. He is the first to open the doorway that leads to the Father (John 17:5, 11, 21-26). Our prayers enter the spiritual portal of faith that was created and formed by him (John 1:1-3, 12-13). The name of Jesus is the key or password into the presence of God as God's children.

Through this Spiritual connection, he is capable of lifting us up, giving us hope and meeting our needs. This Spiritual connection gives us access into the many biblical promises that God envisions for us.

We need Jesus, and all he stands for to survive spiritually, emotionally, physically and intellectually for he is our God.

Jesus prayed a prayer, just a little before he was to be sentenced to death. He knew he would end up being with his Father, again. He is the mediator between God and man.

*Jesus prayed, "I have glorified thee on the earth: I have finished the work which thou gave me to do. And now, O Father, glorify me with thine own self with the glory which **I had with thee before the world was**. …. Holy Father, **keep them** through <u>thine own name</u> those whom thou hast given me, that they may **be one as we are**. …**Now I come to thee**; and these things I speak in the world, that <u>they</u> might have **MY JOY** fulfilled in themselves. … **keep them from the evil.** Father, I will that they also, whom thou hast given me, **be with me where I am**; that they may **behold the glory** which thou hast given me: for thou loved me before the foundation of the world. …**And I have, declared unto them thy name**, and will declare it: that **the love wherewith thou hast loved me may be in them, and <u>I in them</u>** (John 17:4-5, 6, 11, 13, 15, 24, 26)."*

If Jesus can be in two places at once, so can we because we are connected through him.

God raised us up with Christ and <u>seated</u> <u>us</u> <u>with him</u> <u>in</u> <u>the</u> <u>heavenly</u> <u>realms</u> in Christ Jesus …. For through him we have access to the Father <u>by</u> <u>one</u> <u>Spirit</u> (Ephesians 2:6, 18).

I confess that the name "Jesus" belongs to me and it joins me with my creator. It doesn't matter the difference in time and space in the realm of the Spirit.

Holy Spirit, you are my special guest. For I know that you reside within me. I want to acknowledge you within my life with kindness. You are my comforter, counselor, advocate and teacher, and I thank you that I can talk to you at any moment in time. Realizing that you dwell within me gives me peace of mind!

God, you have lifted my spirit by your Spirit that resides within me, and you have seated me with Jesus Christ in the heavenly realms (Ephesians 2:6). I know my spirit is directly connected.

I also know that the name Jesus is special and powerful. It pertains to all the bible promises of life and godliness. The blessed life is laid up for me to access now. As Jesus is now, so am I, even in this world (1 John 4:17). In Christ, I can have abundant life in every area of my life (John 10:10).

I have been sealed with the Holy Spirit of promise (Ephesians 1:13). The law of the Spirit of life in Christ Jesus <u>has made me free</u> from the law of sin and death (Romans 8:2). I choose to live within that freedom.

Protection

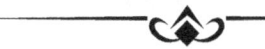

I come boldly to the throne of grace, that I may obtain mercy and find grace to help in times of need (Hebrews 4:16). I can speak for my own life and others with the approval, right and authority, in Jesus' name, because it is the will of God that none perish (2 Peter 3:9).

I agree with God's word by confessing it. It produces life and Godliness. I can decree a thing, and it shall be established (Job 22:28). I can have what I say, bad or good. I can bind bad thoughts and loose God's good thoughts by speaking.

For the record, God does not want to hear what the devil says for he knows already. So don't bind God with bad confessions. Self-pity, sorrow and other negative emotions never release faith.

We should not establish unproductive thoughts and words for ourselves. Don't say, it is not going to work, even if we think it. Bad statements are like weed seeds. They choke out the good that we are trying to plant for our future. Bad statements can keep us from reaching our full and fruitful potential.

Devils believe that there is one God and are very afraid. I submit to God and resist the devil and he will flee.

As I draw near to you God, I know that you draw near to me (James 2:19, 4:7-8).

The joy of the Lord is my strength (Nehemiah 8:10). I can speak good things. I can smile rather I feel like it or not. I can even laugh at the devil to counteract his negative thoughts. I give praise to God above all else, for his joy gives me strength.

God's Word is my confession. I state that the law of the Spirit of Life in Christ Jesus has made me <u>free</u> from the law of sin and death, Romans 8:2.

Let the redeemed of the Lord <u>say so</u>, whom he hath redeemed from the hand of the enemy (Psalms 107:2). I proclaim that I am redeemed from the hand of the enemy. I decree my loved ones redeemed from the hand of the enemy. No evil will befall us, neither shall any plague come near our dwelling. For you Father God, have given your angels charge over us. Your angles keep us in all our ways. In our pathway is abundant life, protection, healing and health (Psalms 91:10-11, Proverbs 12:28).

Angels are ministering spirits sent forth to minister for us who are heirs of salvation (Hebrews 1:14). I stand on this promise from God. For his angels hearken unto his will that none of his perish. I can speak to and send angels forth to perform the will of God for my life, or any of my loved ones.

I confess that I am redeemed and protected from all parts of the curse (Galatians 3:13-14). As Jesus is <u>now</u>, so am I in this world (1 John 4:17). I have been grafted into the kingdom of God and have access to the blessing (Deuteronomy 28:2-13). I live in and have a right standing with my God through Jesus Christ. I take part in the covenant that is paid for through his blood sacrifice that saves me.

Thank you, Father, Son and Holy Spirit for the redeeming blood covenant.

Wisdom, Understanding, Prosperity

God is the giver of all wisdom and all understanding. Prosperity is the result of his wisdom, and understanding.

*Blessed is those who find <u>wisdom</u>, those who gain <u>understanding</u>, for she, (wisdom) is more profitable than silver and yields better returns than gold. She is more precious than rubies; nothing you desire can compare to her. <u>Long life is in her right hand</u>; in her <u>left hand are riches and honor. Her ways are pleasant ways, and all her paths are peace. She is a tree of life to those who take hold of her;</u> **those who hold her fast will be blessed** (Proverbs 3:13-18, also in Proverbs 1:2, 2:6).*

God gave Solomon great wisdom and under-standing. His wisdom excelled the wisdom of all the children of the east country, and all the wisdom of Egypt. For he was wiser than all men ... and his fame was in all nations round about. All the kings of the earth sought his presence just to hear the wisdom that God had put in his heart (1 Kings 4:29-31).

He was happy to spread the wonderful wisdom that God had given him to all who wanted it, and because of his great wisdom, others gave him great riches. Solomon surpassed all the kings of the earth in riches and wisdom. (2 Chronicles 9:1-28).

Jesus tells us to give and it shall be given (Luke6:38). God sometimes uses what we have to give, to give us something else that we need or want.

Here are three miracles where wisdom was involved:

> Jesus feeds 5000 with a very small portion of food that was given to him from a young boys' lunch. (Matthew 14:16-21).
>
> Elijah, the prophet had no food or water because there was a drought in the land. He was sent by God to a widow and her son, who were about to eat their last meal. She gave the prophet some food first, before herself and her son. She did it out of kindness, as well as desperation. She believed him to be God's prophet and that God sent him to her. They both ended up benefiting from the miracle.

God kept the oil and flour in a continued supply to feed all three of them until the drought was over (1 Kings 17:7-16).

Elisha helps a widow who was about to lose her two sons to slavery, in order to pay her creditors. She only had a small jar of olive oil to work with.
He told her to collect as many jars as she could from her neighbors and she did. He told her to pour from her small jar of olive oil into the borrowed jars, and she did. As she poured from the small jar of olive oil, it never ran out of oil. She filled all the jars she could get. She ended up having enough oil to sell and get out of debt (2 Kings 4:1-7).

Jesus, Elijah and Elisha knew what to do, in order for their miracle to come to pass. The young boy with the lunch and the two desperate women took part in a supernatural miracle. They had all accepted God's wise instructions, and it made a huge difference in their lives and the lives of others.

If we are willing to give, share, plant or sow any part of ourselves, like our love, our voice, our belongings, our time, our counsel or our money, God considers it a sweet-smelling sacrifice for his kingdom. If we give what we can to those in need of what we already have, we will lack nothing. If we lend to another without requiring payback, the Lord will be the one who pays us back in one way or another (Proverbs 19:17, 28:27). Give and it shall be given (Luke 6:38).

Lord, I pray your will for my life. I ask for your wisdom and understanding. Please guide me with your wisdom in <u>every</u> situation. For your word says that those who hold fast to wisdom will be blessed. Give me a deep understanding and a compassionate heart for others. Help me make wise choices, and give me instructions for miracles.

I ask to be blessed more like you blessed Abraham, David, Solomon and Jesus. They lacked nothing. They had no issues with being givers. They had more than enough to sustain life for themselves and the lives of others.

Your word promises that you give the ability to produce wealth in order to establish your covenant (Deuteronomy 8:17-18).

Your word says you love a cheerful giver (2 Corinthians 9:7), and I realize that giving goes much deeper than just financially giving. You said to do unto others as I would have them do unto me (Matthew 7:12). You also said do not judge or condemn, but to love and forgive. You said to give and it shall be given, and whatever measure I use, it will be measured to me (Luke 6:36-38).

I delight myself in you Lord, and you give me the desires of my heart…, Psalms 37:4-9. God, I am affirming what you say in your word. You said, "For I know the plans I have for you, plans to prosper you and not harm you, plans to give you hope and a future" (Jeremiah 29:11). Lord, I see that this is your will and your desire towards all your people.

Thank you for your word that gives me hope. I am determined to stand strong and steadfast upon your promises for my life.

You promise that if I seek first the kingdom of God and righteousness, all the things that I need will be added (Matthew 6:33). (I don't need to worry about tomorrow.) Please be totally magnified in my life, for I know that you take pleasure in my success.

First Fruit of the Spirit

Jesus was the <u>first</u> of a new creation for mankind, when he rose from the dead (2 Corinthians 15:3-4). He was the first to be set free from the curse and prison of death, and given eternal life and divine favor.

But now is Christ risen from the dead, and become the "firstfruits" of them that slept. For since by man came death, by man came also the resurrection of the dead. For as in Adam all die, even so in Christ shall all be made alive (1 Corinthians 15:20-22).

The first man, Adam was made a living soul; the last Adam was made a quickening spirit. ... The first man is of the earth, earthly; the second man is the Lord from heaven (1 Corinthians 15:45,47).

Jesus is referred to as the "firstfruits" that rose up from the ground. He was the first of the new creation in the New Testament (1 Corinthians 15:20). He is associated with the "firstfruits" offerings of the Old Testament.

There were many kinds of offerings listed in some of the different books of the bible. The offerings could consist of corn, wheat or barley, wine, oil, honey, fruits, meats, and so on.

For example, the offering could be a small portion of the newly planted grain that came up out of the ground. This small share of the grain was offered to God for his use in the temple, and for his use among the people. In turn, God promised to give them an abundant harvest.

God promised that he would open the windows of heaven to pour out such a blessing, that there would not be enough room to receive it. And, he would protect their crops from being destroyed. Their crops would flourish (thrive, increase, multiply) into a bountiful harvest, all because of the firstfruit offering they gave him. (Malachi 3:10-11). God used the offering to bless the rest of their crops, as well as benefit his people overall.

Their offering involved him in their harvest. It gave him permission to act as a co-owner, or partner in the care of the whole thing. It assured that their remaining grain would be blessed.

God's will for us all is to be fruitful, multiply, fill the earth and subdue it. He loves us and wants us to prosper and be in good health. He wants to bless us in all things.

In the New Testament, God sent a part of himself here to become one of us. When he sowed his Seed in the womb of an earthly woman, he made mankind co-owner of his newly born Son.

Jesus was born Son of God, as well as a son of mankind. He shared in God's DNA. He was the best of two realms and the hybrid of a new kind.

His life, death and resurrection has caught the attention of the whole world. When the world sacrificed him and cut him off from the rest of the living, he was buried in a tomb. **After he was raised up out of the ground through the Holy Spirit, he ascended up to his Father.** This is one of the most well-known stories that the world has ever heard.

Jesus was sent to give us a love relationship with our maker. But he had to do it by way of death first, in order to get it for us. Paul said, that which we sow is not given new life except it die first (1 Corinthians 15:36). Jesus could have called on thousands of angels to rescue him, but he didn't (Matthew 26:53-54). He and his Father loved us that much. They went through the most horrific event that could happen between Father and Son to prove their love for us.

If the devil would have known God's plan, he would not have convinced others to crucify Jesus (Matthew 16:21-23, Luke 22:3-6). When mankind crucified him, they had no idea that they were following God's plan all along (1 Corinthians 2:7-8).

Jesus was meant to be the perfect firstfruit offering of love between God and mankind. He was made up of God's substance mixed with human DNA. The world had to give up Jesus, so that God could get back that part of himself and, to give us new life.

It gave God great joy to see his mortal earthly Son become immortal and imperishable, when he was raised from the dead. God was well pleased to accepted his cross-breed Son, when he accepted Jesus in his own home. God now has blood ties with mankind. Jesus was the best present that anyone could have ever given God.

Except a corn of wheat fall into the ground and die, it abideth alone: but if it die, it bringeth forth much fruit (John 12:24).

So now, because of the birth, life, death and resurrection of Jesus, the <u>firstfruit promise</u> can come to life in the rest of mankind itself (Malachi 3:10-11).

Our Father promises that he would open the windows of heaven and pour out such a blessing, that there would not be enough room to receive it. He did, when he gave us his Holy Spirit!

He also said that he would protect our lives from being destroyed. He did, when he gave us eternal life.

We gave God something to work with when we gave him his Son. He said all our good works would flourish, thrive, increase and multiply, all because of the firstfruit offering he now has from us. It is the greatest offering ever given to God, the Father.

God gives us wealth and good fortune in order to spread his message around the world (Deuteronomy 8:18). He is not finished with his plan, and he wants us to be a part of it all. We are co-owners with God in his efforts to create the biggest and best harvest in our world, all because of Jesus (Mark 4:14-20, 26-32, 34).

Man was first formed from the dust of the ground. Then God breathed into him and he became a living soul. Our bodies, our containers, will return back to the dust of the ground when we die, and the spirit of life will return back to God who gave it (Genesis 2:7, 3:19, Ecclesiastes 3:20, 12:7).

Jesus said that he goes to prepare a place for us in his own Father's house of many mansions (John 14:1-3). The whole process of death has changed since the <u>Holy Spirit raised him to new life</u>, and took him to Heaven. Jesus went to secure our future. He went to secure our citizenship in Heaven (Philippians 3:20). Our destiny and destination have been put in the hands of Jesus.

If we accept this same Holy Spirit that raised Jesus from the dead for ourselves, the real you and me that is in the shell of a body, will have somewhere safe to go when we die. The Holy Spirit knows the how and where in getting us there, since he already did it for Jesus. We, the real you and me go to be with him. Eventually, we will have bodies made like his already glorious body (Philippians 3:20-21).

We must believe Jesus to be the Seed and Son of God. We must believe that he was crucified, laid in the ground, and then rose to new life.

It is interesting to know, that the whole process concerning God's seed was similar to the process of the new grain. Where do you think the grain process and seed comes from in the first place?

The whole **process** regarding the planting of seeds for the grain harvest, led to the **process** regarding the birth, death and resurrection of Jesus. The **process** itself played a part in God's plan to resurrect mankind, and for the record, Jesus was referred to as the bread of life. He said so himself (John 6:35, 47-51).

It is all a matter of accepting Jesus Christ as the firstfruit offering of a new and improved human being, and **letting God become co-owner in our own lives**. We must also believe that when we physically die, like him, we will raise to new life. We didn't initiate the process, God did!

For God so loved the world that he gave his only begotten Son, that whoever believes in him shall not perish, but have eternal life (John 3:16).

Something good was released into our realm or atmosphere that could change the hearts of mankind, when Jesus ascended into Heaven. The Spirit of the Lord is everywhere, and looks into everything, and everybody (Psalms 139:1, 7-8, 1 Corinthians 2:9-10). The Holy Spirit is the giver of God's gift of new life, love and blessing!

Romans 8:9-39 mentions a lot about God's Spirit. The Spirit of God and the Spirit of Christ can live within us (Romans 8:9-11, 14). The Spirit raises from the dead (Romans 8:11). We receive the Spirit of adoption to be God's children (Romans 8:15-17). We have the firstfruit of the Spirit (Romans 8:23). We have the Spirit that helps us pray (Romans 8: 26).

The love of God is shed abroad in our hearts by the Holy Spirit (Romans 5:5).

The Holy Spirit is the blesser that is given to us. He is not a thing. He is a person of the trinity. He is the presence of the Lord God himself!

Flesh gives birth to flesh and Spirit gives birth to spirit. You must be born again of his Spirit. You must be born again of his imperishable seed (John 3:3-6, 1 Corinthians 2:12, 15:42, 1 Peter 1:23-24).

Let God's eternal presence dwell within you and you can live forever. This is what being born again means.

When we accept Jesus Christ for everything he went through and did for us, we make God co-owner over our lives. It is accomplished by his Holy Spirit who comes to live within us. God can bless our efforts, our finances, our health and everything else that we live for, from the inside out. Through him, we can now take part in divine favor, protection and eternal life.

The Holy Spirit knows the mind of God and he knows what's in our hearts. He knows how to intercede on our behalf (Romans 8:26-27).

In the Old Testament, when the firstfruit offering was given, it was actually putting God's principle to work. The priest would take the small bundle of grain and wave it before the Lord. This process was referred to as the "waving of the sheaves". **It was a <u>thanksgiving offering or process</u>**.

The firstfruit offering and feast were celebrated in the spring, at the beginning of the grain harvest. It was a cycle in time to be mindful and thankful for God's provision for the past and the future.

"Firistfruit" in Hebrew means "promise to come". You must believe in this principle regarding the firstfruit offering of thanksgiving. You must believe this principle or process for your own self.

Gratitude and prayerful thanksgiving are necessary in our walk with God. It is our spiritual offering to him, now that the promise of the Holy Spirit has come to live in us. We must be thankful that he made us his children. Showing gratitude is a way of offering our love back to him as our own Heavenly Father.

We can offer praise and thanksgiving to God for our own past and future, just by talking with him. God would be happy to know that we care what he does for us. Even though we now have the Holy Spirit that was promised, there is more to come in our futures!

We have the promise and fruit of the Spirit living within us. We don't have to go through an earthly priest to give God a thanksgiving offering in prayer, even though we could. We can show are appreciation to the Father through his Spirit that dwells within us.

The fruit of the Spirit is summed up in this:

The fruit of the Spirit is love, joy, peace, longsuffering (forgiving, tolerant and patient)**, gentleness, goodness, faith** (and faithfulness)**, meekness, temperance** (having self-control)**: against such there is no law (Galatians 5:22-23).**

The fruit of the Spirit is the perfect qualities of a grateful heart. **This was, and is Jesus!** If we want God's attention, we need to show him are best, a grateful heart like his Son.

God wants us to live with a grateful heart! He wants us to show others a grateful heart!

He has good reason!

The secret and miracle of a seed is multiplication. If we plant a flower seed in the ground, it will flourish into a beautiful flower. If we talk to it, it will enhance the process. That beautiful flower can produce seeds that can eventually become more new beautiful plants. The same goes for fruit and fruit trees. Something in the flower or fruit is capable of producing more like itself. And sometimes it could use some encouragement and love to flourish. It is a supernatural and spiritual phenomenon.

Jesus used parables to teach others about the kingdom of God (Mark 4:2-8, 11, 14-20, 28-29, 30-32). He compared it to literal seed and harvest time. He said that a mustard seed is the smallest seed, yet when it is sown, it grows up and becomes greater than all herbs with great branches (Mark 4:31-32).

Jesus, is referred to as the true vine of God and that we are the branches. We have been grafted in. If we are his branches, we can bear much fruit. If Jesus is holy, and we are rooted in him, we are also considered holy (John 15:1-5 and Romans 11:16-17). The branch's holiness and survival come from being connected to the vine. Jesus is our source for life, health and prosperity.

Jesus is now at the right hand of the Father making intercession to the Father for us. Nothing shall be able to separate us from his love. His love has been planted in us by the Holy Spirit. We have the connection. In all things we are more than conquerors, because of him (Romans 8:34, 35, 37-39).

God, I thank you that Abraham's covenant of blessing includes me and my loved ones, for we have been redeemed and grafted in as your people through Jesus Christ.

Thank you that we have a part in your kingdom blessings, in the name of, and because of Jesus (Galatians 3:14, Romans 11:17). Thank you for giving us power to get wealth. May our wealth and prosperity be multiplied and help in establishing your covenant and kingdom (Deuteronomy 8:18).

I give you a thanksgiving offering of love for everything you have done, are doing, and will do in my future.

Thanksgiving can mean to bless. I bless you God as I give you praise (Psalms 34:1).

I give you praise, honor and thanks for you are an awesome and good God.

I know that the key to the blessing for my own life is through giving good in everything I do and speak. Bad does not work towards the good, but good does!

I thank you for loving me and for going through the pangs of death for me. I thank you for giving me eternal life.

I thank you for comfort, peace, food and shelter, and for blessing me with my family and my children.

Whatever I have, you share with me, and own with me.

I believe in your promise to open the windows of heaven to pour out your many blessings through your Spirit.

All my good works will prosper, thrive, increase and multiply according to your will and promise.

I remind myself to have a grateful heart like the perfect qualities of Jesus. The fruit of the Spirit is love, joy, peace, and longsuffering. Longsuffering is forgiveness, tolerance and patience towards others. The fruit of the Spirit is gentle. The fruit is made up of goodness, faithfulness, humbleness and has self-control (Galatians 5:22-23).

I pray that these qualities of your promised Holy Spirit be instilled in me as I say them.

I pray, that no corrupt communication proceed out from me, only that which is good to the use of edifying for myself and others (Ephesians 4:29).

Doing good is a process that can increase something good.

Dear Lord, I pray that the world I create for myself is good and pleasing in your sight!

(There so many things to be thankful for. Give God a thanksgiving offering of gratitude from your own heart. It is the best thing that you can do with the love between you and God. It is the best way to show him your love for him)

Stopping the Voice of debt

Jesus, you said that if I have faith as small as a mustard seed, I can <u>say</u> to the mulberry tree or the mountain, be uprooted or removed and be planted in the sea, and it will obey me (Luke 17:6 and Mark 11:23). This means that I can uproot or remove things from my own life. I believe your word is true. I accept it in my heart. And, I speak to the mountain or tree that is in my way of prosperity.

If we could, why would we want to uproot a tree or even move a mountain? Would it be to get it out of our way? Is debt something that gets in the way of our prosperity?

Debt has a voice and it speaks to us in many ways. There are words and numbers that can identify or represent themselves as debt. We can either gather together all the paper bills into one pile, and/or summarize the debt on one document with one grand total. We can then use the bill and grand total as a <u>point of contact</u> to remove the actual debt. Think about it as being similar to the mulberry tree. After all, paper is created from trees.

Paper or digital documents that represent debt can scream at us and get in the way of our prosperity.

Previously, I said that things can be multiplied or diminished by using a point of contact to release faith. The woman with the health issue, Elisha, Elijah, the two widow women, and Jesus, all used a point of contact to receive their miracle. Regarding debt, we can prayerfully release our faith, when we touch the bill as a point of contact, and speak to it to be paid in full.

If we also honor God with the first fruits of our prosperity, he promises that our own storehouses will be filled to overflowing (Proverbs 3:9, Malachi 3:10-11, Deuteronomy 28:1-14).

If we can believe God at his word, we can end up with more than enough. With God's accepted process for the firstfruit offering in the Old Testament, we can expect a bountiful harvest in our finances.

Angels are ministering spirits sent forth to minister for us who are heirs of salvation (Hebrews 1:14). They can work behind the scenes where we can't. Angels hearken to the will of the Lord. We can send them to bring in the needed finances to pay a debt or cancel it.

As the needed funds start flowing in, we can take the responsibility of applying it to the debt. In turn, more needed funds can continue to flow in until all is paid in full. It is all in the process. We can keep the flow going!

Debt cancellation can also happen miraculously and instantaneously, like in the story of Jesus and Peter having to pay taxes. Jesus told Peter to go fishing, and the first fish that he was to catch, he would find a piece of money. It would be enough to pay their taxes, and it was!

I have been redeemed from the curse of poverty, and I have a God given right to the abundance of the blessing (Galatians 3:13-14). So, I speak to you, debt, be paid in full! Be uprooted from my life and be no more. Ministering spirits, angels of God, go forth and make it so, for it is the will of God for my life.

I decree that my bank accounts, reserves and other substances overflow in a continuous flow of wealth, so that I have more than enough for myself and others. Prosperity, be a blessing in my life.

I delight myself in you Lord and you promise to give me the desires of my heart… (Psalms 37:4-9). God you said

in your word, "For I know the plans I have for you, plans to prosper you and not harm you, plans to give you hope and a future" (Jeremiah 29:11). Thank you for voicing your words in the bible, for they are my point of contact with you, and I stand firm upon your promises for my life.

Health and Overall Well-being

Obviously, our bodies are capable of being healed; they can and do heal themselves. They use preprogrammed instructions to act out the process for healing. But there are times when the body needs a little help from another source.

We have access to different types of help through taking medicines, receiving some kind of treatment, and through more natural remedies. There are also hidden gems in the bible that are supernaturally inspired by God to help us. Kind words and a cheerful heart are said to be good medicine (Proverbs 12:25, 17:22). They help in the healing process.

God gave King Solomon great wisdom and understanding, as well as a compassionate heart. (1 Kings 4:29-31). Solomon tells us to **keep words of wisdom within our hearts, for they are life and health. He says to guard our hearts above all else, for everything good flows from it** (Proverbs 4:20-23). He also said that we should keep our mouths free of perversity and corrupt talk, and, we should give careful thought to the paths for our own feet (Proverbs 4:24-26). According to his wise advice, whatever we do, hear and speak affects our health.

We should not only take good care of our bodies by exercising and eating the right nutrients, but should also do the same for our spirit man. It is just as important since it affects the whole person too!

Words have a tremendous effect on our relationship with others, but they can also have a life changing effect on our overall health.

The tongue of the wise is health (Proverbs 12:18), and, if anyone can control his tongue, he has perfect control over his body (James 3:2). Wise words can be used to release healing virtue to all parts of the body.

Faith in Jesus Christ makes healing and eternal life available to us. He redeemed us from the curse of sickness, disease, and even death.

Christ hath redeemed us from the curse of the law, being made a curse for us: for it is written, cursed is every one that hangs on a tree: that the blessing of Abraham might come on the gentiles through Jesus

Christ; **that WE might receive the promise of the Spirit** through faith (Galatians 3:13-14).

Jesus said, "The **Spirit of the Lord is upon me, because he hath anointed me** to preach the gospel to the poor; he hath sent me to heal the brokenhearted, to preach deliverance to the captives, and recovering of sight to the blind, to set at liberty them that are bruised (Luke 4:18)."

<u>**God anointed Jesus**</u> of Nazareth <u>**with**</u> the <u>**Holy Ghost and with power:**</u> who went about doing good, and healing all that were oppressed of the devil; for God was with him (Acts 10:38).

There is a real power, influence and authority in Gods words of wisdom. We have a God given right to eternal life, as well as good health, right now! It is God's will for our lives because his words of wisdom say so.

When we speak it to ourselves, healing virtue can flow out from his Spirit into our spirits, and into our hearts. It is his will for us to be healed and we are expected to take care of our health.

A cheerful heart is good medicine, but a crushed spirit dries up the bones (Proverbs 17:22).

Anxiety weighs down the heart, but a kind word cheers it up (Proverbs 12:25).

Encouraging one's self is important in fixing a broken spirit that makes one sick. This applies to all areas of life regarding our overall well-being. When we start to feel anxious about anything, the bible tells us that we should take control over it. What we speak can affect the overall health for our bodies, minds and spirits. This is a spiritual law or principle that works in all aspects of life.

A kind word cheers up the heart (Proverbs 12:25). It is good medicine for all physical and emotional ailments including depression, fear and addiction.

What we think and say are important to our overall health. Jesus said that a good man speaks good things from the heart. Every idle word that men shall speak; they will give account for what they say on the day of judgement. Jesus said by our words we will be justified or condemned. This principle is active today, so we should speak good things (Matthew 12:35-37).

Remember that if anyone can control his tongue, he has perfect control over himself and able to bridle his whole body (James 3:2). We don't always know how or what to speak to improve our quality of life. But we can use God's inspired words as a point of reference. We can speak them directly into our hearts and minds as many times as needed. We can speak until we know, believe and trust our own spoken words. If we know and speak God's will for our own lives enough, what we speak will affect our whole being in every way.

Jesus told us to give, and it shall be given (Luke 6:38). The word "give" covers a broad spectrum of meaning. It means to; freely offer for a purpose, pass it on, to present, freely transfer, cause or allow someone or something to have, hand over to someone else, put in God's care and trust.

Our voice has power! We can give voice to the promises of God in our own lives to be happy and healthy. When we think and speak good things, healing virtue flows (Proverbs 4:20-23).

Remember that the women with the issue of blood thought and spoke what she was hoping for, as she made the connection with Jesus (Mark 5:24-34, Luke 8:42-48).

A wise tongue (or words we speak) can <u>bring</u> health (Proverbs 12:18). Remember that quantum entanglement is where a group of particles interact or share proximity as one, even when separated by a vast distance. It doesn't matter the location, or difference in time and space. We can influence, inspire or cause different parts of our bodies to respond, connect or accept God's healing virtue.

It is God's will and desire to give us quality of life. We should tell him what we need or want, and we should make a statement to ourselves of what we want. We should speak to our bodies regarding health and healing. Words from our own mouths can become a point of contact with God to receive healing and keep healthy.

I have control over my life by what I say and do. I want and need to always control my tongue to speak good things. It is what brings me the good things for my mind, body and spirit (James 3:2).

The tongue of the wise brings health (Proverbs 12:18).

A cheerful heart is good medicine, but a crushed (or broken) spirit dries up the bones (Proverbs 17:22).

Anxiety weighs down the heart, but my kind word cheers it up (Proverbs 12:25).

God, you are my leader, protector and comforter, and I thank you for giving me citizenship status to heaven (Ephesians 2:19-22, Philippians 3:20). Thank you that Jesus' status is released to me and I am blessed. As Jesus is now, so am I in this world. Thank you that you value me as you do Jesus. I know that my bodily presence will be conformed to his glorious body in my future (Philippians 3:21). My life is connected with, entangled with, and sealed as inseparable by your Holy Spirit of promise (Ephesians 1:13).

Father, I believe that your own Word had become flesh as the man Jesus, speaking for you (John 1:1, 14). I confess that you have already sent your Word to heal me by way of Jesus (James 1:21, Psalms 107:20, Proverbs 13:3).

Jesus took my infirmities and bore my diseases so I don't have to (Matthew 8:17). I have been redeemed from all parts of the curse through the blood covenant.

I confess, I am redeemed! I believe and accept this promise for myself.

Lord, your word says that you give me abundant life (John 10:10). I believe and confess that your divine lifeforce flows within me. It brings healing to every fiber of my being. Abundant and infinite life, flow to every organ of my body to keep me in good health.

No evil will befall me, neither shall any plague come near my dwelling. For you Father God, have given your angels charge over me. Your angles keep me in all my ways. In you, I have abundant life, protection, and good health (Psalms. 91:10-11, Proverbs 12:28).

I speak the same thing over my loved ones. I plead your blood covenant and promise of healing for their lives. (Say their names).

Jesus, you tell us to heal the sick, cleanse the lepers, raise the dead and cast out devils: freely I have received, freely I give (Matthew 10:8, Luke 10:9). In Jesus name, I pray that your life-giving force flows within them and brings healing to every fiber of their being, as they need it. The kingdom of God is all about the abundant life. Abundant life, flow to every organ to keep them in good health.

I speak the word of God over them. No evil will befall them, neither shall any plague come near their dwelling. For you Father God, have given your angels charge over them. Your angles keep them in all their ways. In you, they have abundant life, protection, and good health (Psalms. 91:10-11, Proverbs 12:28).

I speak to apply your healing virtue to myself, mind, body and spirit. I believe that healing is flowing throughout my bloodstream to all parts of my body, as I speak. My blood has the right chemical balance for life and health. My redeemed blood flows to every cell restoring and transforming my body for new life.

I declare, that the word and wisdom of God is manifesting itself and flows throughout my body. I plead the blood covenant over my own life, and Father, through your Word, your Son, you have imparted new life to me. That life restores my whole body, mind and spirit with every breath I breathe, and every word I speak. You took my infirmities and bore my sickness. Therefore, I refuse to allow sickness to dominate my body.

Body, I speak the word of faith to you, for you are the temple of God's Spirit (1 Corinthians 3:16 and 6:19). Heart be and stay strong and perfectly whole. I declare, my blood pressure is perfect and my arteries are clean and elastic as they should be. Body, release the right chemicals. Be in perfect chemical balance. God who dwells in you wants you well.

I declare sickness, fear, depression and harmful addictions have no power over me. God's Word is my confession, and I am free from the law of sin and death in Jesus' name.

I confess that healing belongs to me. I have no abnormal growths, tumors or arthritis. Cancer cannot exist in my body or my presence. Pancreas, secret the proper amount of insulin for life and health. Liver, lungs, endocrine and digestive systems, kidneys and vascular circulation systems function properly. Skin and hair be youthful and healthy. Teeth and gums be healthy and strong. Hearing and eye sight be perfectly whole. Spine, bones and joints be perfectly healthy and function properly. Body, I speak to you, maintain proper posture. Brain and mind be healthy in tissue and in thought. I live in and have a right standing with God through Jesus Christ. Therefore, I am healthy!

Jesus, you said, "Ask what you will, and it shall be done to you" (John 15:17). I believe and trust you at your word. Thank you that I am redeemed from any part of the curse. Your word is alive and active in me! I will not die but live and declare the works of God (Psalms 118:17).

I pray for my loved ones that healing, health and abundant life flows through them. They too will not die, but live and declare the works of God (Psalms 118:17).

Reveal your love to them! I pray that they get a revelation knowledge of who you really are, and how much you love them.

Thank you, Jesus Christ, for dying for me and my loved ones, so that we can live forever. Thank you for your promise that says to ask and it shall be done.

The abundant life that comes from you as my risen savior, resides within me and I in you. I have been redeemed. You promised to always lead me into triumph as I follow you (Galatians 3:13-14 and John 15:17). I trust you with my life!

I say and pray all in Jesus Name, Amen!

Affirmations

Giver of Life

Father, I believe that you are the one who gives us all things richly to enjoy, for you are the giver of life (1 Timothy 6:17.

I thank you Father for all your promises. For no matter how many promises that you made, they are "Yes" in Christ" (2 Corinthians 1:20).

God's Faith Works by Love

Faith is the substance of things hoped for, and it works by love. (Hebrews 11:1 and Galatians 5:6).

The <u>love of God</u> has been poured out in my heart by the Holy Spirit who was given to me. (Romans 5:5). God gave me his Love. God loves me!

The fruit of the Spirit is love, joy, peace, longsuffering, gentleness, goodness, faith, meekness, temperance: against such there is no law (Galatians 5:22-23).

I allow God to work in and through me by the fruit of his Holy Spirit.

God's love for me and in me is what activates faith for all good things (John 14:6, 12-18, 21-23).

Thank you, Jesus for I can follow your example of how faith works! Love and faith go hand in hand!

Love has a Voice

Love is <u>patient</u>, love is <u>kind</u>. It does <u>not envy</u>, it does <u>not boast</u>, it is <u>not proud</u>. It does <u>not dishonor others</u>, it is <u>not self-seeking</u>, it is <u>not easily angered</u>, it <u>keeps no record of wrongs</u>. Love does <u>not delight in evil</u>, but <u>rejoices with the truth</u>. Love <u>always protects</u>, always <u>trusts</u>, always <u>hopes</u>, always <u>perseveres</u>. ...And now these three remain: faith, hope and love. But the greatest of these is Love (1 Corinthians 13:4-8, 13).

Love had a voice and it made a difference! The perfect love of God and his Son Jesus was faultless and unselfish! If God the Father and his Son Jesus took it upon themselves to love us, we ought also to love one another (1 John 4:9-11). Love has a voice and it makes a difference!

There is no fear, (or anxiety) **in love, and perfect love casts out** (forcibly expels or dismisses) **fear (1 John 4:18).**

I can do the two greatest commandments to love God above all and secondly my neighbor. The life I now live is by faith in Jesus Christ that is in me. I have the greatest love residing within me. I can do all things through Christ who loves and strengthens me" (Philippians 4:13, Galatians 2:20).

Words are Carriers of Power

I thank you, God for your word! Your word shall not return to you unfulfilled, but will accomplish that which you please, and achieve the purpose for which you sent it.

According to your word, I ask that <u>your words that I speak</u> accomplish what I desire, and that it achieve the purpose for which I send it (Isaiah 55:10-11).

Jesus, you said that you came so that I can have life more abundantly (John 10:10). You also said that you are the vine and I am the branch. If I remain in you and you in me, I will bear much fruit like a tree with its branches. If I remain in you and your words remain in me, I can ask whatever I wish and it will be done (John 15:1-7).

I give human voice to God's sayings, just like you, Jesus! I know that my giving voice to God's words links me to him through you. What I say shall accomplish that which I please. It shall prosper in the thing that I send it, because it was, and is, God's words first.

I believe that sound waves are powerful when given substance, direction and instructions. They can create change.

I know that I can speak or give voice to receive what I need and even want for God loves me and wants me blessed.

God is able to bless me abundantly, so that in all things at all times, having all that I need, I will abound in every good work (2 Corinthians 9:8). In you Jesus Christ I have abundant life (John 10:10).

Every time I speak words of faith to make changes in my life, it creates a stronger image or imprint inside me, as I hear myself speak. The more I speak it, the more it is polarized and energized, until I know that I know. What I say sets up my future.

Life and death are in the power of the tongue. I choose to speak life (Proverbs 18:21).

A gentle and wholesome tongue is a tree of life, but willful words spoken against the word of God, breaks down the spirit (Proverbs 15:4).

I keep or guard my mouth and tongue, for it keeps my soul from trouble (Proverbs 13:3, 21:23).

I strive to let no corrupt communication proceed out of my mouth, but that which is good to the use of edifying, that it may minister grace unto the hearer (Ephesians 4:29).

My desire is to speak things that edify and improve my life and the life of others.

I am reminding myself to put a watch on what I say, and always strive to speak in love. I choose to speak words of life!

I create the fruit of my lips. I shall be satisfied with good, by the fruit of my mouth (Proverbs 12:14).

I remind myself that all words are seeds that produce something. Good seeds produce good results.

Father, I confess and believe that your spiritual kingdom principles, your powerful life-giving seeds, are available to my spirit from yours (Luke 8:11-18). I confess that the Word of God is alive, living in me! For words are living things!

Out of the abundance of my heart my mouth can and wills to speak good things (Luke 6:45). All good things come from you, God.

Just like you did Jesus, I want to plant good spiritual seeds of love to reap good result. You said that you are in your Father, you are also in me and I am in you (John 14:16 and 20, Ephesians 3:17, Galatians 2:20, 4:19). You said we are connected as one together, so I can speak the will of our Father for my life to reap good results

I confess that as I walk in your ways Lord God, you make my way plenteous in goods, you open your good treasure, you bless all the work of my hand and I can lend to others and not have to borrow for myself (Deuteronomy 28:9-12).

Thank you for your words that give blessing to my life.

Envy Gets in the Way of our Peace.

Regarding envy, I choose to change the outcome for good in any bad situation. Someone else's circumstance does not dictate my future, I do! Envy will not rule over my feelings, I will! I will to make envy of no affect in my life or another by doing the right thing. I rule over it according to Genesis 4:7 because God said I could. I plan to keep my feelings of love, peace and joy and be happy.

Forgiveness

For though I live in the world, I do not wage war as the world does. The weapons I fight with are not the weapons of the world. <u>They have divine power to demolish strongholds</u> (2 Corinthians 10:3-4).

I demolish arguments and every pretension that sets itself against my mind, and the knowledge of God. I place these thoughts into captivity to the obedience of Christs (2 Corinthians 10:5).

Forgiveness is part of God's covenant with me. God forgave me and so I choose to forgive!

I choose to bring thoughts of unforgiveness and blame of another into captivity. I move forward out from any bondage. I take back my freedom from an unproductive situation. I respond back with God's divine power that demolishes strongholds. I choose forgiveness and it sets my emotions free.

Making Change for the Better

God, your word says to let the people praise you, then shall the earth yield her increase and you shall bless them. I praise you God as my own God. I believe in your word that says you shall bless me (Psalms 67:5-6).

Blessed be your name Lord for you hear the voice of my supplications. You are my strength and shield. I engage in and soak up your perfect and holy presence. I become strong in your strength. I trust in you, and I am helped. My heart greatly rejoices as I give you praise for all you do.

I want to think, speak and do the right thing, in order to affect my life, and the life of others for the better. I want to influence others to have good thoughts about me. I want to live in your blessing and not in the curse

Save us as your people, bless us as your inheritance, feed and lift us up together forever (Psalms 28:7-9).

Quantum Entanglement

I confess that the name "Jesus" belongs to me and it joins me with my creator. It doesn't matter the difference in time and space in the realm of the Spirit.

Holy Spirit, you are my special guest. For I know that you reside within me. I want to acknowledge you within my life with kindness. You are my comforter, counselor, advocate and teacher, and I thank you that I can talk to you at any moment in time. Realizing that you dwell within me gives me peace of mind!

God, you have lifted my spirit by your Spirit that resides within me, and you have seated me with Jesus Christ in the heavenly realms (Ephesians 2:6). I know my spirit is directly connected.

I also know that the name Jesus is special and powerful. It pertains to all the bible promises of life and godliness. The blessed life is laid up for me to access now. As Jesus is now, so am I, even in this world (1 John 4:17). In Christ, I can have abundant life in every area of my life (John 10:10).

I have been sealed with the Holy Spirit of promise (Ephesians 1:13). The law of the Spirit of life in Christ Jesus <u>has made me free</u> from the law of sin and death (Romans 8:2). I choose to live within that freedom.

Protection

I come boldly to the throne of grace, that I may obtain mercy and find grace to help in times of need (Hebrews 4:16). I can speak for my own life and others with the approval, right and authority, in Jesus' name, because it is the will of God that none perish (2 Peter 3:9).

I agree with God's word by confessing it. It produces life and Godliness. I can decree a thing, and it shall be established (Job 22:28). I can have what I say, bad or good. I can bind bad thoughts and loose God's good thoughts by speaking.

Devils believe that there is one God and are very afraid. I submit to God and resist the devil and he will flee. As I draw near to you God, I know that you draw near to me (James 2:19, 4:7-8).

The joy of the Lord is my strength (Nehemiah 8:10). I can speak good things. I can smile rather I feel like it or not. I can even laugh at the devil to counteract his negative thoughts. I give praise to God above all else, for his joy gives me strength.

God's Word is my confession. I state that the law of the Spirit of Life in Christ Jesus has made me <u>free</u> from the law of sin and death, Romans 8:2.

Let the redeemed of the Lord <u>say so</u>, whom he hath redeemed from the hand of the enemy (Psalms 107:2). I proclaim that I am redeemed from the hand of the enemy. I decree my loved ones redeemed from the hand of the enemy. No evil will befall us, neither shall any plague come near our dwelling. For you Father God, have given your angels charge over us. Your angles keep us in all our ways. In our pathway is abundant life, protection, healing and health (Psalms 91:10-11, Proverbs 12:28).

Angels are ministering spirits sent forth to minister for us who are heirs of salvation (Hebrews 1:14). I stand on this promise from God. For his angels hearken unto his will that none of his perish. I can speak to and send angels forth to perform the will of God for my life, or any of my loved ones.

I confess that I am redeemed and protected from all parts of the curse (Galatians 3:13-14). As Jesus is <u>now</u>, so am I in this world (1 John 4:17). I have been grafted into the kingdom of God and have access to the blessing (Deuteronomy 28:2-13). I live in and have a right standing with my God through Jesus Christ. I take part in the covenant that is paid for through his blood sacrifice that saves me.

Thank you, Father, Son and Holy Spirit for the redeeming blood covenant.

Wisdom, Understanding, Prosperity

Lord, I pray your will for my life. I ask for your wisdom and understanding. Please guide me with your wisdom in <u>every</u> situation. For your word says that those who hold fast to wisdom will be blessed. Give me a deep understanding and a compassionate heart for others. Help me make wise choices, and give me instructions for miracles.

I ask to be blessed more like you blessed Abraham, David, Solomon and Jesus. They lacked nothing. They had no issues with being givers. They had more than enough to sustain life for themselves and the lives of others.

Your word promises that you give the ability to produce wealth in order to establish your covenant (Deuteronomy 8:17-18).

Your word says you love a cheerful giver (2 Corinthians 9:7), and I realize that giving goes much deeper than just financially giving. You said to do unto others as I would have them do unto me (Matthew 7:12). You also said do not judge or condemn, but to love and forgive. You said to give and it shall be given, and whatever measure I use, it will be measured to me (Luke 6:36-38).

I delight myself in you Lord, and you give me the desires of my heart…, Psalms 37:4-9. God, I am affirming what you say in your word. You said, "For I know the plans I have for you, plans to prosper you and not harm you, plans to give you hope and a future" (Jeremiah 29:11). Lord, I see that this is your will and your desire towards all your people.

Thank you for your word that gives me hope. I am determined to stand strong and steadfast upon your promises for my life.

You promise that if I seek first the kingdom of God and righteousness, all the things that I need will be added (Matthew 6:33). (I don't need to worry about tomorrow.) Please be totally magnified in my life, for I know that you take pleasure in my success.

First Fruit of The Spirit

God, I thank you that Abraham's covenant of blessing includes me and my loved ones, for we have been redeemed and grafted in as your people through Jesus Christ.

Thank you that we have a part in your kingdom blessings, in the name of, and because of Jesus (Galatians 3:14, Romans 11:17). Thank you for giving us power to get wealth. May our wealth and prosperity be multiplied and help in establishing your covenant and kingdom (Deuteronomy 8:18).

I give you a thanksgiving offering of love for everything you have done, are doing, and will do in my future.

Thanksgiving can mean to bless. I bless you God as I give you praise (Psalms 34:1).

I give you praise, honor and thanks for you are an awesome and good God.

I know that the key to the blessing for my own life is through giving good in everything I do and speak. Bad does not work towards the good, but good does!

I thank you for loving me and for going through the pangs of death for me. I thank you for giving me eternal life.

I thank you for comfort, peace, food and shelter, and for blessing me with my family and my children.

Whatever I have, you share with me, and own with me.

I believe in your promise to open the windows of heaven to pour out your many blessings through your Spirit.

All my good works will prosper, thrive, increase and multiply according to your will and promise.

I remind myself to have a grateful heart like the perfect qualities of Jesus. The fruit of the Spirit is love, joy, peace, and longsuffering. Longsuffering is forgiveness, tolerance and patience towards others. The fruit of the Spirit is gentle. The fruit is made up of goodness, faithfulness, humbleness and has self-control (Galatians 5:22-23).

I pray that these qualities of your promised Holy Spirit be instilled in me as I say them.

I pray, that no corrupt communication proceed out from me, only that which is good to the use of edifying for myself and others (Ephesians 4:29).

Doing good is a process that can increase something good.

Dear Lord, I pray that the world I create for myself is good and pleasing in your sight!

(There so many things to be thankful for. Give God a thanksgiving offering of gratitude from your own heart. It is the best thing that you can do with the love between you and God. It is the best way to show him your love for him)

Stopping the Voice of Debt

Jesus, you said that if I have faith as small as a mustard seed, I can <u>say</u> to the mulberry tree or the mountain, be uprooted or removed and be planted in the sea, and it will obey me (Luke 17:6 and Mark 11:23). This means that I can uproot or remove things from my own life. I believe your word is true. I accept it in my heart. And, I speak to the mountain or tree that is in my way of prosperity.

I have been redeemed from the curse of poverty, and I have a God given right to the abundance of the blessing (Galatians 3:13-14). So, I speak to you, debt, be paid in full! Be uprooted from my life and be no more. Ministering spirits, angels of God, go forth and make it so, for it is the will of God for my life.

I decree that my bank accounts, reserves and other substances overflow in a continuous flow of wealth, so that I have more than enough for myself and others. Prosperity, be a blessing in my life.

I delight myself in you Lord and you promise to give me the desires of my heart... (Psalms 37:4-9). God you said in your word, "For I know the plans I have for you, plans to prosper you and not harm you, plans to give you hope and a future" (Jeremiah 29:11). Thank you for voicing your words in the bible, for they are my point of contact with you, and I stand firm upon your promises for my life.

Health and Overall Well-being

I have control over my life by what I say and do. I want and need to always control my tongue to speak good things. It is what brings me the good things for my mind, body and spirit (James 3:2).

The tongue of the wise brings health (Proverbs 12:18).

A cheerful heart is good medicine, but a crushed (or broken) spirit dries up the bones (Proverbs 17:22).

Anxiety weighs down the heart, but my kind word cheers it up (Proverbs 12:25).

God, you are my leader, protector and comforter, and I thank you for giving me citizenship status to heaven (Ephesians 2:19-22, Philippians 3:20). Thank you that Jesus' status is released to me and I am blessed. As Jesus is now, so am I in this world.

Thank you that you value me as you do Jesus. I know that my bodily presence will be conformed to his glorious body in my future (Philippians 3:21). My life is connected with, entangled with, and sealed as inseparable by your Holy Spirit of promise (Ephesians 1:13).

Father, I believe that your own Word had become flesh as the man Jesus, speaking for you (John 1:1, 14). I confess that you have already sent your Word to heal me by way of Jesus (James 1:21, Psalms 107:20, Proverbs 13:3).

Jesus took my infirmities and bore my diseases so I don't have to (Matthew 8:17). I have been redeemed from all parts of the curse through the blood covenant. I confess, I am redeemed! I believe and accept this promise for myself.

Lord, your word says that you give me abundant life (John 10:10). I believe and confess that your divine lifeforce flows within me. It brings healing to every fiber of my being. Abundant and infinite life, flow to every organ of my body to keep me in good health.

No evil will befall me, neither shall any plague come near my dwelling. For you Father God, have given your angels charge over me. Your angles keep me in all my ways. In you, I have abundant life, protection, and good health (Psalms. 91:10-11, Proverbs 12:28).

I speak the same thing over my loved ones. I plead your blood covenant and promise of healing for their lives. (Say their names).

Jesus, you tell us to heal the sick, cleanse the lepers, raise the dead and cast out devils: freely I have received, freely I give (Matthew 10:8, Luke 10:9). In Jesus name, I pray that your life-giving force flows within them and brings healing to every fiber of their being, as they need it. The kingdom of God is all about the abundant life. Abundant life, flow to every organ to keep them in good health.

I speak the word of God over them. No evil will befall them, neither shall any plague come near their dwelling. For you Father God, have given your angels charge over them. Your angles keep them in all their ways. In you, they have abundant life, protection, and good health (Psalms. 91:10-11, Proverbs 12:28).

I speak to apply your healing virtue to myself, mind, body and spirit. I believe that healing is flowing throughout my bloodstream to all parts of my body, as I speak. My blood has the right chemical balance for life and health. My redeemed blood flows to every cell restoring and transforming my body for new life.

I declare, that the word and wisdom of God is manifesting itself and flows throughout my body. I plead the blood covenant over my own life, and Father, through your Word, your Son, you have imparted new life to me. That life restores my whole body, mind and spirit with every breath I breathe, and every word I speak. You took my infirmities and bore my sickness. Therefore, I refuse to allow sickness to dominate my body.

Body, I speak the word of faith to you, for you are the temple of God's Spirit (1 Corinthians 3:16 and 6:19). Heart be and stay strong and perfectly whole. I declare, my blood pressure is perfect and my arteries are clean and elastic as they should be. Body, release the right chemicals. Be in perfect chemical balance. God who dwells in you wants you well.

I declare sickness, fear, depression and harmful addictions have no power over me. God's Word is my confession, and I am free from the law of sin and death in Jesus' name.

I confess that healing belongs to me. I have no abnormal growths, tumors or arthritis. Cancer cannot exist in my body or my presence. Pancreas, secret the proper amount of insulin for life and health. Liver, lungs, endocrine and digestive systems, kidneys and vascular circulation systems function properly. Skin and hair be youthful and healthy. Teeth and gums be healthy and strong. Hearing and eye sight be perfectly whole. Spine, bones and joints be perfectly healthy and function properly. Body, I speak to you, maintain proper posture. Brain and mind be healthy in tissue and in thought. I live in and have a right standing with God through Jesus Christ. Therefore, I am healthy!

Jesus, you said, "Ask what you will, and it shall be done to you" (John 15:17). I believe and trust you at your word. Thank you that I am redeemed from any part of the curse. Your word is alive and active in me! I will not die but live and declare the works of God (Psalms 118:17).

I pray for my loved ones that healing, health and abundant life flows through them. They too will not die, but live and declare the works of God (Psalms 118:17).

Reveal your love to them! I pray that they get a revelation knowledge of who you really are, and how much you love them.

Thank you, Jesus Christ, for dying for me and my loved ones, so that we can live forever. Thank you for your promise that says to ask and it shall be done.

The abundant life that comes from you as my risen savior, resides within me and I in you. I have been redeemed. You promised to always lead me into triumph as I follow you (Galatians 3:13-14 and John 15:17). I trust you with my life!

    I say and pray all in Jesus Name, Amen!

www.ingramcontent.com/pod-product-compliance
Lightning Source LLC
Chambersburg PA
CBHW031653040426
42453CB00006B/287